"As a Chicano by culture, I ha~~ ~~hop-
ing a young latino/a jaguar a   e
luke-warm room temperature p   :ry
from wedding cake Poet Laureat   v
pleased I was when I read Lu   1
the literary sense, it combines to create unique voice, **its images are vital to the context of our age** and it has a strenuous if not desperate sense of trying to make sense of the chaos, the violence, the racism, the lies....

I look forward to seeing the progressive development of this wonderful poet..."

Jimmy Santiago Baca
Winner of the Pushcart Prize, American Book Award, National Poetry Award,
the International Hispanic Heritage Award, and the prestigious International Award

"**The voice of Warrior-Poet of the Fifth Sun is a compelling and desperately needed one. The words - intrinsically beautiful in their own right - speak to important political and social issues.** López moves smoothly from the Chicano to the Brown to the Latino to the Human experience. He is able to explore these identities in great depth with simple carefully crafted phrases. The pages of this book advance through different styles, as stream of consciousness meets hip-hop meets the etechnology of our time. The emotional range - from exuberance to melancholy - make the reading an exhilarating experience. Anger turns to joy which turns to sadness as the reader turns the pages. The work is inspirational. Through his poems, López tells his distinctive story - yet the words resonate from so many perspectives that the poems invite readers to interpret their own individual experiences through them. **This multivocality makes the book a must-read for anyone interested in exploring identity. Powerful!**"

James Vreeland, Ph.D.
Department of Political Science
Yale University

"**Warrior-Poet of the Fifth Sun** is an eloquent collection of poems that captures a rare view into the imagination and reality of a modern day poet. Lopez's debut work describes the joy, love, and pain of urban life and how his world exists beyond the physical one. His prose is full of a vibrancy and passion that bring to life this body of work. **The power of his expression weaves the ancient and contemporary, unifying the worlds that divide and unite America.**"

Reymundo Dominguez, Ph.D.
University of Southern California

"**At once encompassing the context of 2nd generation Chicanos and beyond** - to indigenous bloodlines of the past, Luis López transitions from the historic then to the personal in this beautiful book of prose regarding what it is to be Chicano in 2004. Not afraid to venture away from the once rigid definition of Chicano, **López shines through as a next generation poet/intellectual with rare insight into the two worlds that we have come to call The Mexican American Experience**. Warrior-Poet of the Fifth Sun is a relevant, joyful read for anyone of any background and race interested in the search for meaning and identity in this paradox we call home."

Carlos Rueda
Philosopher
SJSU

"**When most poets write of their worlds we gain insight into their lives**, but in the end we are left fully aware that in some sense we are voyeurs who will always stand outside the door watching them through the window of their existences. However, **Luis A. López opens the door and invites us into the living room of his soul**, where the words are chiseled with the blood and the tears of three cultures, torn loose and laid before us in a rendering that one marvels at how lines so clean and simple in the end are interweaved in such complexity that for the instant we read them we truly become a part of the world as seen through his eyes. His poems meet the highest criteria of poetry: they are honest, as natural as breath, and offer insights so obvious that the reader wonders why he never thought of life quite in those terms on his own. **These are true poems that speak to the mind, the body, and the soul, as all good poetry should.**"

Roger Humes, Director
The Other Voices International Project

"**Can somebody say, 'Paradigm Shift'?** Mr. López's book of poetry marks a fundamental shift in the field of Chicano studies. Finally, a X-icano poet emerges from the X-generation as true to his 1980's urban American upbringing as to the Mexican roots of his migrant ancestors. **López is that unique poet who's references are a masterful blend of Mexica-Azteca folklore and American pop history**: from Quetzalcóatl and Cuauhtemoc to Jack Kerouac and Grandmaster Flash.

In his work, **Warrior-Poet of the Fifth Sun**, the oh-so talented López courageously takes on formerly taboo subjects such as the Pope, Black-Chicano relations and our love-hate of the Spanish. As you will see from your readings of López, Chicanos can finally boast a homegrown poet with the cross-over appeal of a Selena Quintanilla or an Oscar De La Hoya. **It is now just a matter of time before the Ivy League academics and the MTV generation come to recognize this phenomenal and genuine talent.**"

Albert Jimenez Howell
MTS
Harvard Divinity School

*helio*graphica

AS A RESULT OF THE HELIOGRAPHICA SUSTAINABILITY

PROGRAM, 10 CENTS FROM THE PROCEEDS OF

THIS BOOK WILL BE DONATED TO ENVIRONMENTAL

CAUSES THAT SUPPORT FOREST PRESERVATION AND

ENVIRONMENTAL EDUCATION FOR CHILDREN.

Warrior Poet
of the
Fifth Sun

by Luis A. López

*helio*graphica

Warrior Poet of the Fifth Sun
Copyright© 2004 by Luis A. Lopez

No part of this book may be reproduced or transmitted in any form or by any means, graphic, electronic or mechanical, including photocopying, recording, typing, or by any information storage retrieval system, without the permission of the publisher.

*helio*graphica

For information:
Heliographica
2261 Market St., #504
San Francisco, CA 94114
www.heliographica.com

Library of Congress Control Number: 2004116656
ISBN 1-933037-52-0

Printed in the United States of America

Typeset, Layout, Cover and Poem Page Designs by Ken Machado.
Title Page and Final Page Illustrations by Marty Maaske.

Warrior Poet of the Fifth Sun

by Luis A. López

Note from the Author

I want to thank you from my heart for taking the time to read my words, my poetry.

In today's visually complicated world, poetry has lost its place in society. Poetry has become something we see poorly acted on stage, something we abhor to read, poets have become complacent - poetry is dying a slow painful death.

In the worlds that came before us, poets were celebrated. They were entrusted to be the leaders of their clans, their tribes, their nations. They saw life as it was and captured it in the writers snares. They told stories of life, after-life and stories of gods. They told stories of you. Today's poets count syllables, worry about pentameter, and write for self-glorification. I'm here to wipe that all away, I'm here to open your mind and heart to embrace who you are. I'm here to blow life back into the dying pen of yesterday.

I am a Chicano, I am a Poet. I tried to separate the two, but I couldn't do it. I tried and tried, but my soul wouldn't allow it. The words are fused together as one, and always will be. It is the fabric of my existence. Chicano-Poet is all that I am.

These poems are about life as I know it, from a poet born and raised in San Jo, Califas to Mexican parents - A father who didn't learn english until 15, a mother who spent many nights working in cannery sweatshops. I am the son of revolution, the son of trying times.

I'd like to open this book with a poem from one of my own sons, David Alejandro, my baby, my little flaco. He is 9 now, and wanted to write poems like his father. His words moved me more than anything on this earth. And I am proud, as proud as any man can fathom. My son carries tradition deep within him. It is in his bones.

HONESTY

Honesty is it forgotten?
Honesty is it foreign?
Honesty is it true?
Honest is my tribe
Honest are my people
Honest are my fellow warriors
Honesty is true
Honesty is never forgotten
Honesty is not foreign
-David A. López, 9

I am equally proud of my oldest son, Miguel Desmundo, my little reflection. He has found the magic of music, the other half of me, as his art form. He is studying saxophone, and the new artistry of turntablism -engulfed in the dusty records of old. He, like David, has all of my blessings and support in searching thru this life-dream for his song, his inspiration.

I hope these words touch you.

Thank You,
Luis
http://aztecpoet.com

Dedication

This book is dedicated to my grandfathers, my parents, and to my warrior-sons.

I also dedicate this to my loving grandmothers that guided and taught me, Aurora and Angelita. My angel and my light.

To all of my friends and familia that have supported me over the years. To all the poets that picked me up and shook me to my core.

I'd like to thank Ken Machado for being by my side throughout the crafting of this book. The cover of this book is his art, and I am indebted to him for such a wonderful masterpiece.

Thank you to Marty Maaske for his drawings - the Warrior image for the title page, and the Xochipilli image on the last.

And to David Craig, the teacher that inspired me to write poetry. I still have that poem that you wrote for me Dave, and the spark of creation is still with me. Thank you all.

lyrical, satirical
satori synthesizer
weaver of words webbed welkin
wish on the future
waste not a moment
the spark of creation to stay
dc, 1988

Table of Contents

1. Ode *to* Chichén Itzá
2. The Brown Non-Fiction
3. Pedro
4. Sons *of the* Fifth Sun
5. España
6. Flow
7. You
8. Poet *of the* Red & Black Ink
9. NY, NY Big City *of* Dreams
10. Again
11. Chicano Style
12. Immersion
13. Poet Tree
14. Abuelita

Table of Contents

15	Poetry
16	Re-Verse
17	The P.O.P.E. *is a* P.I.M.P.
18	Dualities
19	Prayer
20	Chant I Am
21	Inter-Tribal Communications (2004)
22	My Home
23	God
24	Nectar
25	Poetic Definition
26	Intentions
27	Manos *de* Maíz
28	Thoughts

Table of Contents

29		Meditations
30		The Tribeless Ones
31		Re-Birth
32		The Angels *that* Surround You
33		Poets
34		Spoken Word
35		We Must Rise Again
36		Grand-Father
37		When I Go
38		Night
39		Alive
40		The Flower *of the* Sun

**Poetry was the only occupation worthy of an
Aztec warrior in times of peace.**

And so I found myself,

without a war.

1. Ode to Chichén Itzá

shadows of the serpent

born of a
sun-moon
kiss

entering you

you
embraced me

my breath
almost
left me

left me
to
breathe
on my own

my search
watched over

the right eye
of
Xaman Ek

sacred quetzál

clapping
their green song
from your
feet

ninety one
steps
of
timeworn indio
clay

climbing on top
of you

half step at
a time

inhaling answers

exhaling
truth

don't let it linger

drink
from this water

where the
wise-men of the water
drink

the sound of the
voice

it surrounds
you
passes through
you
becomes
of
you

Kukulcán
demi-god of lore

charting stars
and
mapping myths

your poem
sculptured
from
mystical
air

angelic whispers
deciphered

under
the watchful eye of the
suns

Warrior-Poet of the Fifth Sun *Luis A. López*

2 | The Brown Non-Fiction

they decided to sell me

again, but not the
same

*no te
alarmes*

It's not so bad like
before

they put me out in the open

my own little
esquina

of the
white page
forest

in between
Kerouac
and
Pablo

aquí 'stoy

leaning right here
on
Montoya

in between
your small cappuccino
and
crumpet

find me

*aquí me
encuentras*

in the nestled cracks
of the
hidden aisle

the one you
always seem

to
pass

'stoy aquí

at the
bottom

reach for me
take me off the shelf

shake off

the dust
of
five hundred years

touch
my hyphenated
binding

duro chicano
cover

with a
soft spanish
lining

they put my section
right on the
border

right there
between spark
and
friction

pick me up
for just a minute

and

fan your face
with my
words

3. Pedro

Warrior-Poet of the Fifth Sun   *Luis A. López*

Pinche Pedro

negrito

why'd you have to go
and die?

You were the one

that always brought a
nuyorican smile
to these tainted
chicano eyes

Remember

selling condoms and poems

fitting all
with one
size

Pietri, hermano
young lord of nueva york

Spitting spanglish
with
ease

Speaking broken
english mas fluently
que me

Birthing your
own

your little
café on the
street
You were able to see
our struggles were
all the same

When I go to spanish harlem
i'll go visit
sister lópez
I heard she still
has reasonable

fees

Maybe i'll get a family discount,
and the vieja will do it for
free

You know I'm hoping
the good news is still
guaranteed

Like you said

Extinction is not on our agenda

You taught us all
so well

Aquí Que Pasó Power is still
what's happening

Aquí to be called negrito
means to be called LOVE

4 Sons of the Fifth Sun

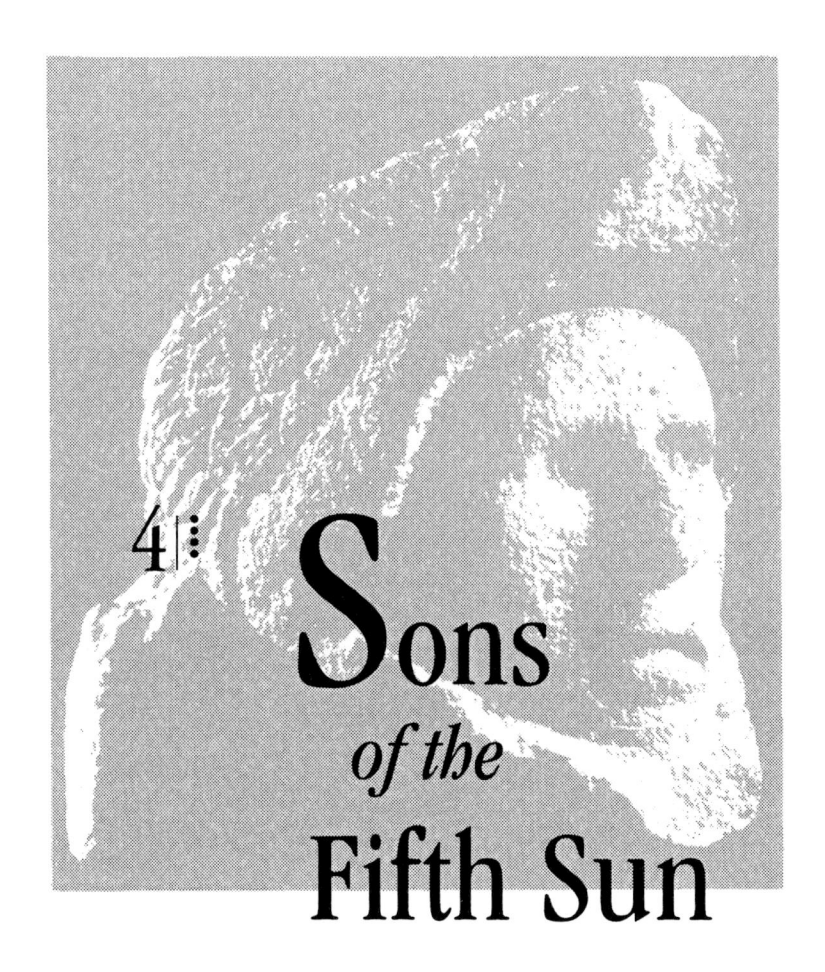

Warrior-Poet of the Fifth Sun   *Luis A. López*

You were born with a
Warrior-heart

A heart that has passed
From generation to generation

It was not I that gave you this gift
Of fire, of anger, of pride, of pain

The gift came from the Mexica, the Azteca
Your grandfathers Quetzalcóatl and Cuauhtemoc
Zapata, Rivera, Villa, Marcos

I was simply the messenger, a conduit
For a life story much older than I

Warrior-Prince by birth
By the blood of your ancestors

The blood shed by the greedy gold digging guns of Cortés
The blood shed by the Christ-less Christians
The blood shed by the lusts of the Pope's Catholic Corporation
The blood shed from field worker's calloused hands
The blood shed from the brave warrior-children of Chapultepec

The blood shed over lands that can never truly be owned

This is the blood that runs through your veins
This is the gift that gave and gives you life
Embrace this
Never dishonor this sacrifice of powerful love

My
Warrior-Sons
Of the fifth sun

You are like the flower, mi'jo
Beautiful, strong, duro - a survivor
As you grow through this life dream
finding the words for your song
your poem
Use these words to shade you
To comfort you to protect you

The blood of a nation courses through your veins

Warrior-Poet of the Fifth Sun   *Luis A. López*

5 España

Warrior-Poet of the Fifth Sun   *Luis A. López*

I grew up in a household
that blamed spain

and everything spanish

for the broken state of our
aztlán nation

the bearded white man from spain
was always the cause

for everything

why did you work in the fields daddy?
why is mommy working in a cannery until midnight papa?

pinche cortés

was a favorite saying of my father

if only he hadn't killed the aztecs
if only he hadn't killed the aztecs

I knew the story as a young boy growing up

they thought he was quetzalcóatl resurrected
and so they trusted him

pinche cortés

when I was young I would ask questions
it's a habit I have yet to break

but papa', aren't we mestizo?
doesn't that mean mixed?
I thought one great-grandfather was a spanish sailor,
a captain?
why does my grandmother have green eyes?
doesn't that mean we have their blood too?
isn't López a spanish name?
You're chicano mi'jo
xicano

You have the blood of the *indio* side mi'jo
your other great-grandfathers and grandfathers
used to wear
flour sacks for pants and a rope for a belt
in the hills of sonora,
and the coast of mazatlán

you are dark like him

ever since i can remember
my mother has always wanted to vacation
in spain
to meet madrid,
to smell the sweet scent of seville
learn flamenco in
barcelona

Warrior-Poet of the Fifth Sun   *Luis A. López*

but my
father refuses to take her
he has no use to see that land he says

*that land that sent the bearded white man and
his horses*

as a boy
we tend
to try and be like our fathers

so I must admit, for a period
I distanced myself from anything spanish

my father says I am chicano,
indio
so in my mind that's what i was

a five foot ten azteca warrior of *puro sangre de indio*

---

today I awoke a bit late
leaning in to my morning
hungover from
a late night

and I read the news
of those poor spanish
people

my people

being blown up for
simply getting on a train
for simply trying to get to work
to feed their families

for trying to live a good honest life

I have no words to convey how i feel

my mestizo blood boils

our family tradition stops
today
mi España

I somehow need to embrace you

forgive me

6 Flow

it used to be that i couldn't write
without a pencil
pens were too messy

being left handed meant
smudged
ink up my hand and arm
ruined cuffs and constant
explanation

then as i began to type
it became more than words

i would catch the rhythm of the keys
my own little drum machine

i didn't care what came out

a little white out and a little patience
went a long way in those days

but that rhythm

that collective fury of
sound

first a beat up IBM selectric
click clack click clack
zzzzzip...
carriage return

then for
christmas a fancy new
word processor

verb puree

I could actually delete before
comitting

and with my
skills
the flow increased

that little rhythm

Warrior-Poet of the Fifth Sun   *Luis A. López*

click clack, clickity clack clack
clickity clack clickity click clack
boom bap boom bapbap

my eyes would roll
back as if
to look at myself
as i lost myself

and i would enter that place
that rhythmic poets place

that place i long for now

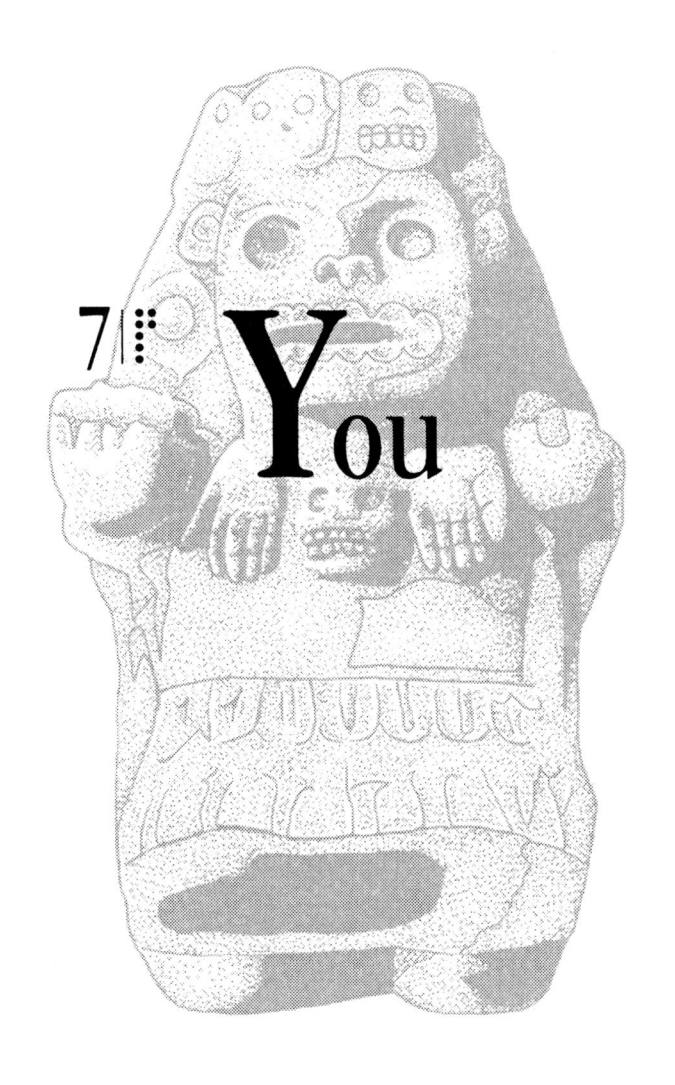

7 You

Warrior-Poet of the Fifth Sun　　　　　　　　　　　　　　　　　　　　　　　　　　　　　　　*Luis A. López*

as We
are
now known
as
I

I
must confess

'twas I
that loved
you

8 | Poet *of the* Red & Black Ink

Words
like strewn arrows

lay about me

reminding me

of the so many marks
missed

of the so many battles
lost

of the so many miscalculations

Where are the
words

that flying true

hit their mark

that ran away
stuck

to their
target

where are the words
that fired
perfectly

the first
time

and penetrated
flesh so
easily

9 Ny, NY Big City *of* Dreams

hip-hop

is what i spray painted
on the fresh new walls of
my jr. high

hip hop

it was a large piece
probably
ten feet

wild style

i remember the red
and yellow paint
running down my
face

b-boy

big bold letters custom
cut

i was out for
fame

puma's looking fresh
with the
fly fleamarket Todd 1's

adidas in the closet
in case of emergency

we all wanted to be in the
rocksteady crew
15 guys named crazy legs at school
g-roc
sir pop-a-lot

i wanted to rhyme with the cold crush
learn to scratch like
Theodore

throw up a burner like zephyr

i even wished i was from the boogie down
to hang with Bam in the park
spin in the streets to that mad new vibe

looking for that perfect beat

we would make mix tapes
with records and
the pause
button on our tape recorders

i used to do that for hours

Roxanne Roxanne
i wanna be your man

mixmaster in the small bedroom
3000 miles from the bronx

i wish i could hear one of those tapes now

i laugh when i think of the
grandmaster flash mixes
i used to carry in my hoodie
like gold

man, hip-hop

a classmates mom saw me mid-masterpiece
and called the cops
i was able to finish it before i ran

whoop,whoop
that's the sound of the police
i got pinched in school on monday

i had to pay for the
re-painting and do
community service to pay for my
crime

but for that brief week it was up

i would marvel at it

in the middle of san josé
i had my very own
New York

10 Again

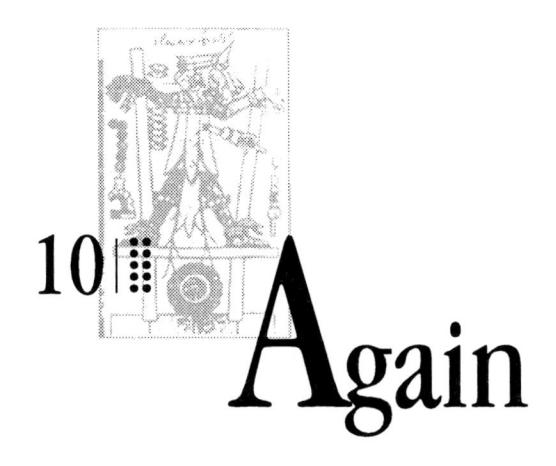

fingers on
fire
ripping
the reigns of
reality
confinement never an
option
let me see you
as you are
not as you want
me to see you

understand

with
what I've seen
how can it matter

I already see
thru you and
your
seven shoddy veils
of poorly controlled
perception

can't you see?

you yourself are
eluding you
of your
very being

little selfless you

11 Chicano Style

Warrior-Poet of the Fifth Sun   *Luis A. López*

i met
another poet
today

i didn't realize there were so many

he spoke to
me about
form and then
he
spoke
to
me
about structure

and he decided to tell
me about poet
after poet
after
poet
and used big sparkly white
fancy words
those words I heard they
sell
at the universities

I didn't realize there were so many

and then
the five dollar
question

he asked
me
in what
did
i consider my style

?

and so
i
considered
it

but i wasn't sure
if
chicano chingon
was a choice

Warrior-Poet of the Fifth Sun   *Luis A. López*

12 | Immersion

As we immerse ourselves
into
the very things
that have become
us
the very things
that became
us
the very things
that we have
become
in spite of
us

I dare to
dream
of movements, of actions
I dare to
dream
of flowers, of blossoming
of defiant eruption
within our,

our collective
soul

or

was that merely another dream

a
dream
of wine, of incense

a
dream
of coalesce?

remind me

tell
me again

show me
why

Warrior-Poet of the Fifth Sun   *Luis A. López*

we have
immersed
ourselves into

the very things
that
have moved
poets
for all time

the very things
that
give life to the
writers pen

As we ourselves emerge
from
the very things
that have become
us
I want to emerge
with you
I want to emerge with
us

only to immerse
myself
in
you

13 Poet Tree

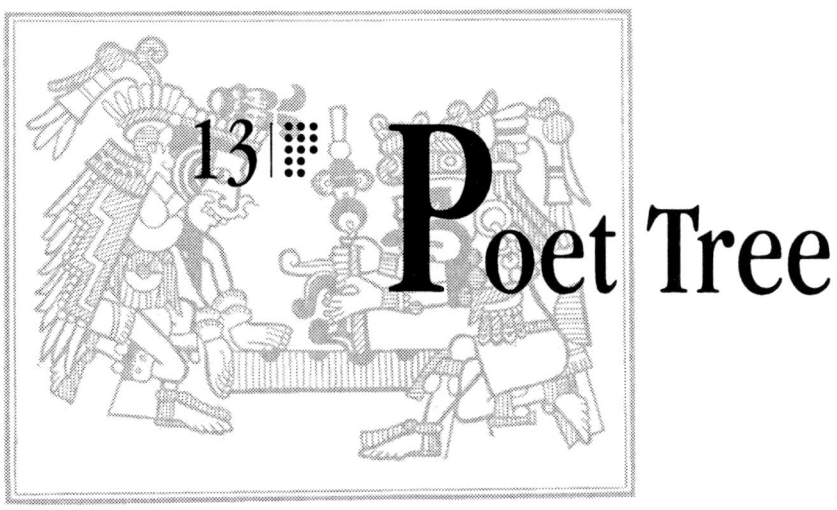

Warrior-Poet of the Fifth Sun   *Luis A. López*

A good friend told me to try Whitman
(that for sure he would change my life)
And so I chose
to read the words
And as I emerged
I was still the same old poet
I jumped in again
And again and again
And still the same
poet of old
Somehow I couldn't get down
with the civil war pains
of the white man's
killing
of the white man
Like the bible,
I
simply couldn't feel
it in my
soul

14 | Abuelita

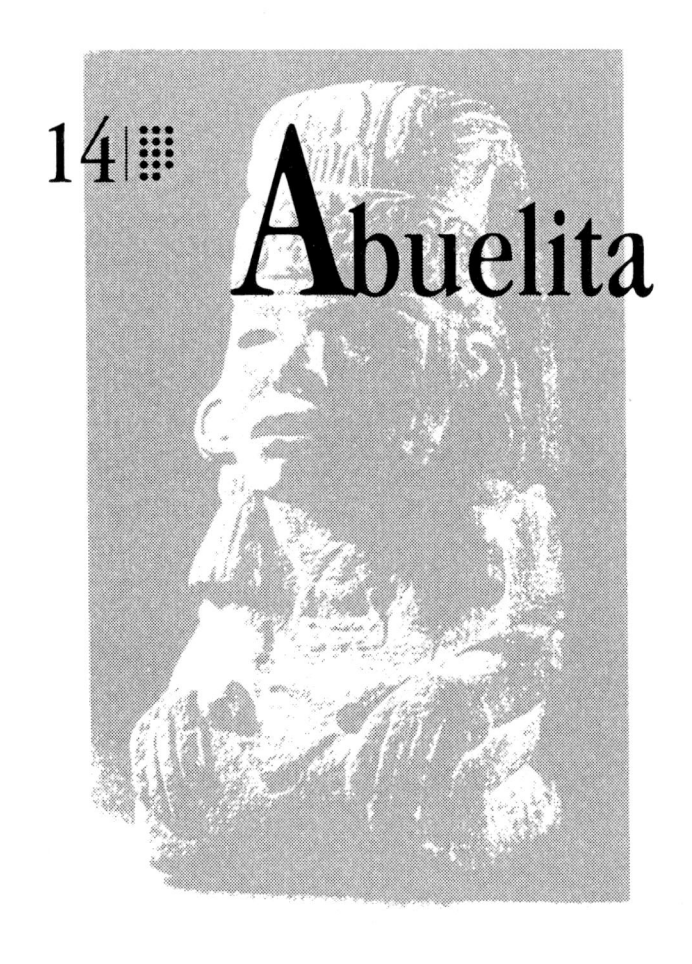

the prints of your fingertips have been
left on my soul
like the stain of a wine red sea

aurora! my heart, my
everlasting song
come home and sing to me

15 Poetry

Warrior-Poet of the Fifth Sun   *Luis A. López*

I hesitate sometimes when I tell people that I am a poet, that I write poetry

The word
somehow does not fit

Poetry.
Poetry?

Where is the word that explains what Bukowski writes?
Where is the word that reeks of Neruda's ode to feet?

Where is the word that raises forth from my soul to shout to the world that
I am the ancient sage of old,
that I bring forth the words that drip
from that place in my darkness,
my light

Where is my word?

16 Re-Verse

Isn't it strange
how sometimes a
poem

has a way
of opening its
penetrating eye

and reading
you?

dark words
on a light
page

gently peel away
your life
masks

exposing and
judging
you

silently

You,

sinner

No?

But, why
do
your hungry
eyes betray
you?

can't you see
their reflection in
this verse?
did you really
think that you could
avoid it?

maybe out
run it,
like you do
your very own
soul?

Warrior-Poet of the Fifth Sun *Luis A. López*

look again

deeper
closer
snuggle up with me

this is not the time to be
shy

like the time
you whispered need
when what
you really meant was
want

like the time
you said forever
and never
meant more than
now

your ego
your lies

your silly
false pride

17 | The P.O.P.E. is a P.I.M.P.

i see
him comin

the m.c. pope

can't you see him from here
with his fat gold rope?

rollin' all slow
in his bullet-proof whip

i don't know if gold means
he's a
blood or a crip

m.c. pope
you had the christians' backs for days

helped invent the drive-by
i think you called 'em crusades

claiming your turf
and holdin' it down

an army of priests
can't wait to get down

spittin' rhymes for people and
taking a
tip

fill 'em with fear
so you dont have to hear any
lip

damn kid
i see your grafitti all over town

but mostly in places
populated by brown

i even live in a city
named after one of your saints
tagged us pretty good with

life-long european paints

Warrior-Poet of the Fifth Sun *Luis A. López*

you got us all mixed up
we don't know who to pray to

burning incense at altars
but on sundays we pay to
see you

m.c. pope

yo son,
your skills i have to admire
my favorite one is

when god sent fire

18 Dualities

spill from
my
lips

and scatter from me

words of the
forked tongues

dueling
for my throat

blood of the
oppressor
and of
the oppressed

within me

english of the queen
español
de su majestad

wrestling for
my mouth

nahuatl
mi campeón

nowhere to be
found

deprived and

left to nourish
on
the fruit of barren
trees

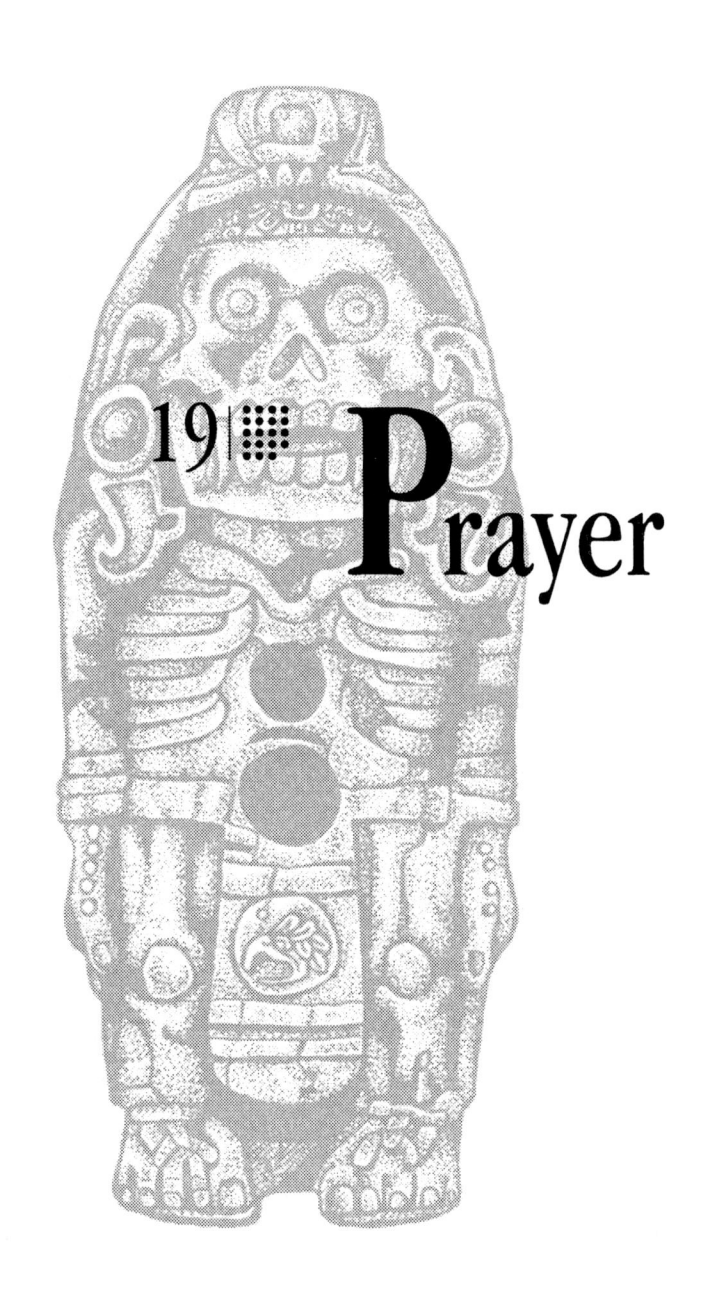

19 | Prayer

dear ometeotl, god, dios, creator, father,
the sun

you know what I mean
it's not your name that matters
when we are two
we are one

there's confusion surrounding us
we've lost the ability to see
my brothers and sisters are lost

help them see you thru me

we're growing so fast, and without any guidance
the flower songs were hidden

we've had to grow in silence

false prophets surround us, no one's making any sense
we're all so confused

your beautiful children sitting
on
barbed-wire fence

forgive us,
we know not what we do

my brothers killing each other
instead of uplifting
to somehow reach
you

please know in the end
that's all we're looking for

the guide the path
the stairs
the door
forgive the mexica, the maya, columbus and cortés

forgive the ones that put your people
out there
on the
rez

forgive religion
the races
slave blood that still drips
all the people brought or conquered by devils
on ships

Warrior-Poet of the Fifth Sun　　　　　　　　　　　　　　　　　　　　　　　　　　　　　　　　*Luis A. López*

forgive the devils too
i dont think they meant so much harm
they got caught up in riches
put us all out on the farm

help them too
because they deserve to see

i have to be truthful
they could have
been me

in today's world our blood is all intertwined
blood of the indio
slowly
erased over time

help quell the battles within us
our mixed blood sometimes boils

we don't know whether to soar like the eagle
or be
like the serpent
that coils

so much noise and pollution inside of us
our minds should be clear
too many eyes
painted with bold strokes of fear

there's so much darkness around
revolution can't see
show us some sort of light

we long to be free

please forgive me father
i've done some god-awful things too

i'm not worried about that now
i'll find the time to have that talk
with you

Warrior-Poet of the Fifth Sun *Luis A. López*

2011 Chant I Am

Warrior-Poet of the Fifth Sun   *Luis A. López*

words i am
water i am
flesh i am

the song of the drum i am

wind i am
vibration i am
truth i am

blood i am
sage i am

heat i am
weaver i am
thought i am

the song of the flower i am

warrior i am

sacred i am
movement i am
voice i am
spirit i am
herb i am

the song of the creator i am

revolution i am
curandero i am
maiz i am
sun i am
battle-cry i am

the song of the earth i am

poultice i am
visions i am
fire i am

alive
i am

Warrior-Poet of the Fifth Sun   *Luis A. López*

21st Inter-Tribal Communications (2004)

Warrior-Poet of the Fifth Sun *Luis A. López*

african_warrior: que doing?
aztec-poet1: nada, coldchillin
african_warrior: orale vato
african_warrior: sup for 2nite holmes?
aztec-poet1: no se, sup?
african_warrior: donde estan los girlies?
aztec-poet1: none here b
african_warrior: pinche poet, no rukas
aztec-poet1: been busy g gotta right this verse
african_warrior: werd handle that shite kid
african_warrior: imma be @ the spot @10
aztec-poet1: mebbe te veo
african_warrior: serio? u better show up nekka
aztec-poet1: werd
aztec-poet1: i'll shoot you a smoke signal when I roll-up
african_warrior: coolio
aztec-poet1: peace
african_warrior: uno

22 My Home

somehow i ended up
in the park

writing again

the park downtown

downtown San José
in Califas

Califas

the heart of Aztlán

César Chávez
parque

museum of arte
on my right

Quetzalcóatl
poised for battle
beside me

in front of a building called
Heritage

here

my words connect to the
world for
free

and yet i still sometimes wonder

if a writer is what i was
destined to
be

23 God

i met god today

he came right up
to me
in the park

i was sitting alone

with my faded
parchment
and
rusted pen

he was a dark man

hair in tangles
shoeless feet

calloused

from giving
himself to the earth

he had this
glow about him

as he asked me for a coin

or at the very least
some change

i was certain
i was out of change

and so i told him
no

i'm sorry but i can't

as he slowly turned away
i could see that his red eyes
were burning

burning with the fire
that
i
seek

so i checked all of my belongings
and i found
not one silver coin
but two

and as he passed again
to give me

my second chance
my redemption

i offered it to him

and that glow
that fire within
his eyes

quickly spread
to his mouth
and surrounded him

it leapt out in bursts
and flicked against my
skin

the flames arose
and entered
me

as he blessed me

and turned
to face his day

24 Nectar

breaking through
the earth

this little
seed

of force

making its way
through black
wet earth

and rock

finding its
sacred place

on this holy ground

to firmly
root
and stand tall

the tools
of thought
and of strength

the tools
to clear the path

instinct

the most treasured
axe

burst forth
and display

your flower

let us taste
of your
nectar

let us see you

as you are

25 | Poetic Definition

i defy you to
define me

put me within your
walls made
by
the hands of
man

tether me to
your
opinion

reign me in
and try to make
me stop

i defy you

with everything
that i am

26 Intentions

who are you
today

as you awake and stretch
into your morning

reflections

of what you are
and who you long
to be

are you

the movement of mountains
this morning

the voice that echoes

or the lifeless leaf
blown
from the tree

does your soul sing the
song of tranquility

or do you sit alone

in the carvings of your
pain

will you move the moveless
minds today?

be fire to the stricken
of doubt

or are you nothing but

intention

the face without
the mouth

Warrior-Poet of the Fifth Sun   *Luis A. López*

27 Manos *de* Maíz

Warrior-Poet of the Fifth Sun   *Luis A. López*

throughout time

your hands
have nourished
us

sustained us

provided without
hesitation

those precious
potent hands

delicately
shaping
us

into the form
of angels

the shapes
of gods

guerreros del sol

the giver of
strength
you
are

from
the grinds of
earth

you emerge

this food of life

in all your
glory

the splendorous one

a pestle
a jarro

Warrior-Poet of the Fifth Sun　　　　　　　　　　　　　　　　　　　　　　　　*Luis A. López*

like swords
by your side

sheathed in
wisdom

warrior in your own
right

your fire
your shielding
comal

stay with us

throughout the
darkness of our
nights

28 Thoughts

as we begin

again

the thoughts of the
omnipotent

the thoughts of the
forebearers

the thoughts of those
that came before us

those voices that
still softly sing
in the
silence of the night

listen

they are asking
to be heard

29 Meditations

Warrior-Poet of the Fifth Sun   *Luis A. López*

Frequently I find myself

I find myself

alone

30 The Tribeless Ones

            i want to become one
               with the earth
                   again

                to let my soul
              mingle with the gods

           i want to pluck the whisker
                 from a jaguar
              in the black stillness

                 of the night

            i want to climb the highest
                    peak
               become like the bird
           and come home triumphantly

                 with the plume
                    of the
                  elusive one

              i want to kneel to
                the wooden sky
           to ensure the corn will grow

              i want to pray for rain

           i want to be a new-born again
                  to be covered
                with sacred maíz

            as a welcoming to this world

              i want to be the mexica
                  percussionist
                the drum that brings
             the sounds from deep within

               i want to pierce my skin
                and let my blood flow
                        be
             the unspoiling honey of the gods

            i want to be the setter of bones
                    the herbalist
                 a shaman to the weak

Warrior-Poet of the Fifth Sun   *Luis A. López*

i want to be the guardian of
culture
the song of the
otherworlds

i want to bring my kill
to the village
and divide it

with my people
of the sun

i want to bring honor
to my family

through the gratitude
of my ways

i want to be harmonious
and never
questioning

i want to be the eloquent one

i want to write this on the wall
with
the instrument of words

i want to smell of the
jungle

those ancient aromas of
the past

i want to sleep in the
hut held up
with
living tradition

the smoke that rises
more than once

31 Re-Birth

Here it will be written
Here it will not be lost again
Here the stories of the ancient ones still burn

We left Aztlán
We left Chicomoztoc

To Anáhuac
To build a nation

We became Mexica
We became Tenochca

We became the flower
and we flourished

The sun has risen again
The drum is sounding
The moon has laid out the path

The time has come for us to return to our home
The time has come for us to return to our land

We have been called back by the earth

Our fathers, grandfathers
and great-grandfathers
call to us

Mexica! Mestizo!

Aztlán!

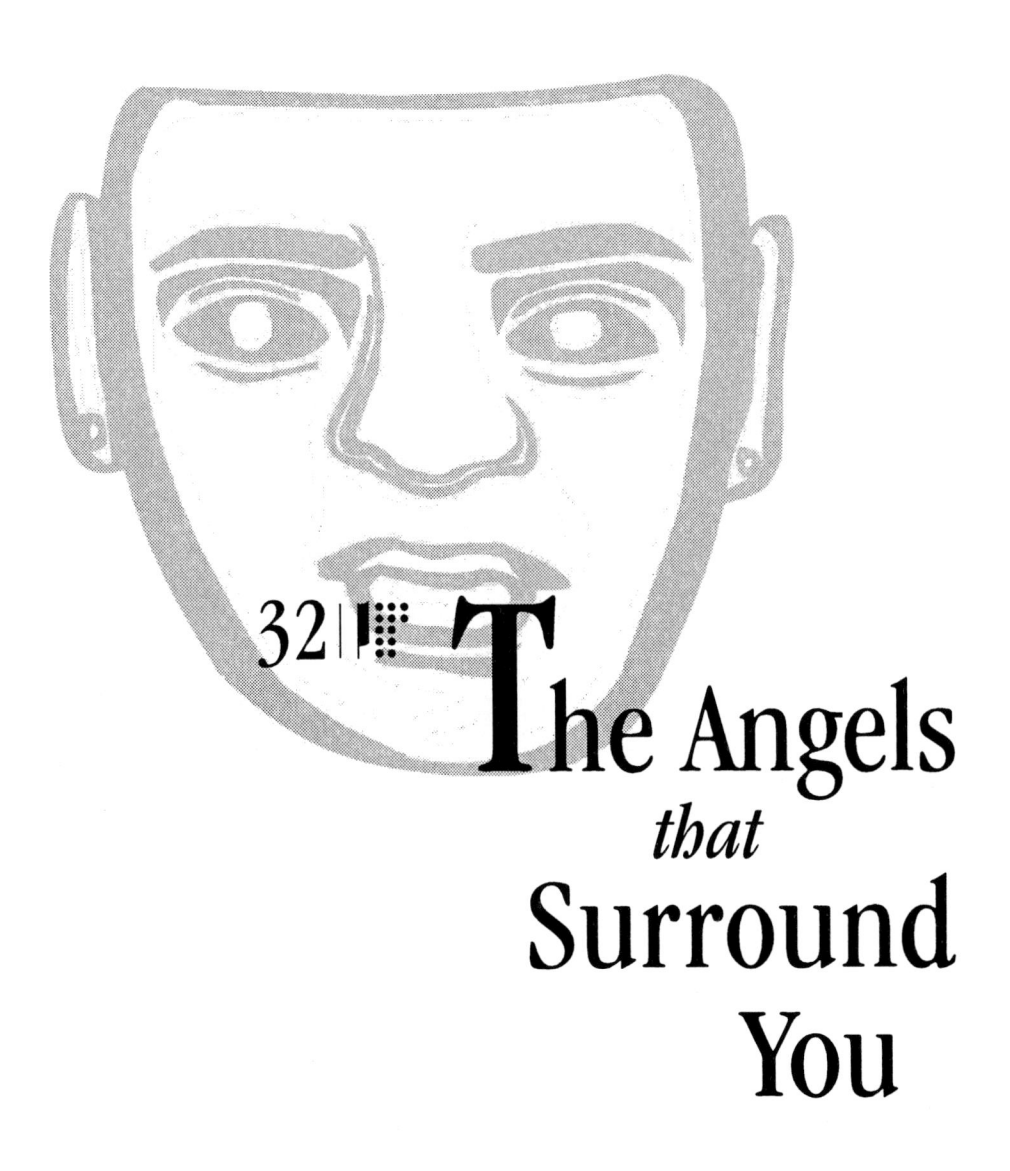

32 The Angels *that* Surround You

Warrior-Poet of the Fifth Sun   Luis A. López

we bless the food
that nourishes you
as we pull it from the earth

we wash your cars and
clean your homes
because we know the gods

require beauty

we raise your children
in your absence

instilling in them culture

we sing them lullabyes of revolution
as we send them peacefully
to sleep

we trim the lawns and rake the leaves
to insure
our mother is respected

there's an army of us

waiting
on you

in front of your stores of home improvement

pick us up and take us home
we'll do whatever it is you ask

we'll bow our heads and
say thank you

gracias

is how our tongues sometimes say it

tonight

before you
lay down your head

you thank your god

for the angels
that surround you

33 Poets

Warrior-Poet of the Fifth Sun   Luis A. López

poets get so caught up
in writing poetry

for poets

they seem to have forgotten
about you

using fingers to count their
syllables

phonetic segments
constant restraint

instead of using thought
to convey their
truths

Who ponders the world
in which we live?

34 Spoken Word

I do the math
and I dont know how

I dont know how
to factor

the poets that
get up on stage
and transform themselves

to actor

I believe in voice
in song in rhyme

in words pointed at the head

But given the choice
I think I'd prefer

to talk with you in bed

35 ▓ We Must Rise Again

Warrior-Poet of the Fifth Sun   *Luis A. López*

we have no honor

nobility
is not ours

we have strayed from the
paths laid out by
our fathers

we have no dignity

we run down the streets
like rabid dogs

graceless

is what we have
become

who is to blame?

no one taught us
to be men

no sacred rituals
no sacred truths

we replace them

with gangs
and thuggery

a machismo
that is false

players
in a game
meant to be lost

never striving to be wise
wisdom erased

infants teaching ourselves
how
to walk

rich history
tossed
to the wayside

knowledge lost

but we are men now

and the burden lies
upon us

the time has come
to right the wrongs

to re-learn the
ways never taught

let us bear this burden
thankfully

and

clear the path
for our children

making way

for a new
sun

36 | Grand-Father

my grandfather was a man
of light

a light that still shines within me

i wear his face
his skin is mine

i carry him
effortlessly upon my back

he speaks to me on the rocks
through the wind that calms
the tide

he has become the root
of my flowers

the one to which i am
in debt

and so i honor him
with words

with the songs
that he planted carefully

inside of me

words of beauty words of strength
words of courage

words of gods

these
are his words

Warrior-Poet of the Fifth Sun   *Luis A. López*

37 When I Go

let the rains come

let the rain
wash me

from this
earthly place

hide my tracks
stifle my scent

smother me in
history

let the water
cleanse me

let the waters guide

38 Night

do we dishonor you?

o, creator!

the
ones among us

with skins of bronze

do we bring shame to your name?

o, creator!

why
do you treat us
so?

look upon us!

we
yearn to see your face

39 Alive

Warrior-Poet of the Fifth Sun   *Luis A. López*

in my veins these
words flow

they pour from me
when i bleed

rhythms of
the creator

rhythms of
the earth

beat within my heart

this blood

that
sustains me

Warrior-Poet of the Fifth Sun   *Luis A. López*

40 The Flower of the Sun

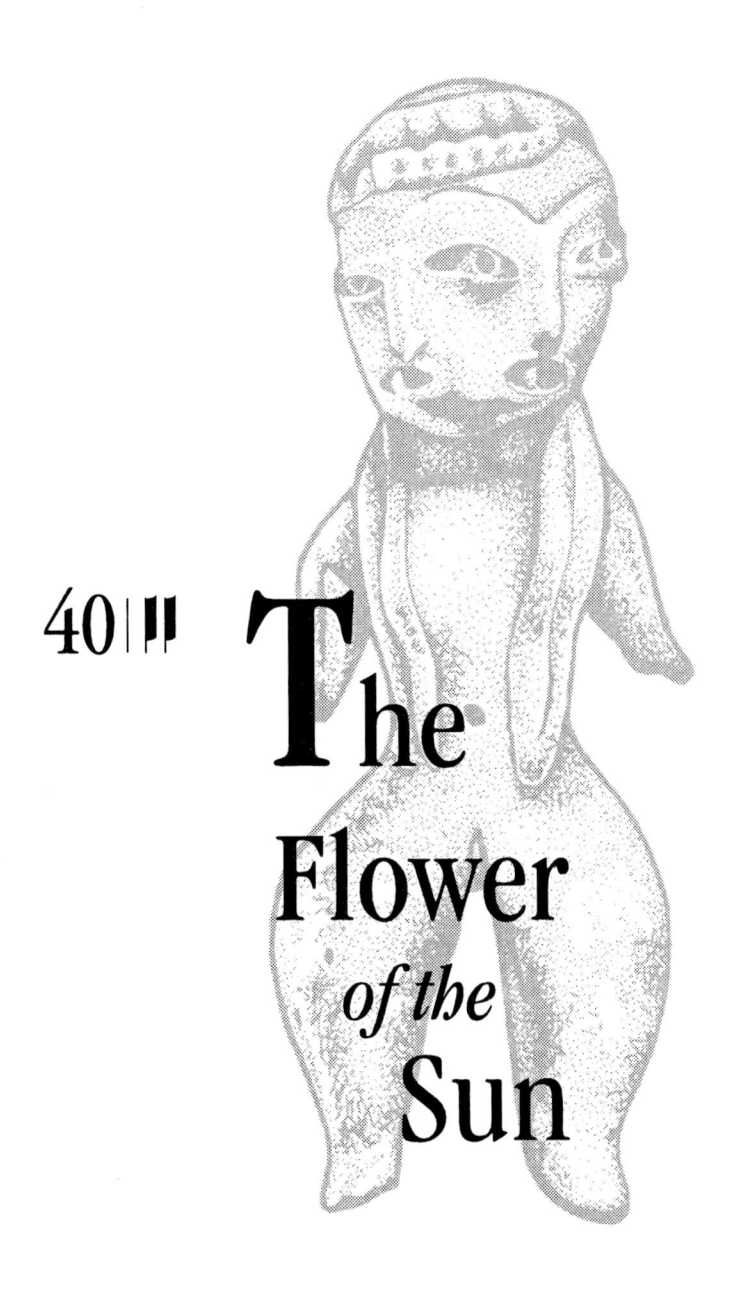

Warrior-Poet of the Fifth Sun   *Luis A. López*

she came to me
like the calmest wind

blowing through me
around me
peacefully

she told me stories of
yesterdays

of nows
of tomorrows

recollections

of all women
past

her black
breath
left shades of
white

a welcome breeze
simplistic purity

a shadow
in which to
shade

her scent was comforting

milky
warmth

a nest for which to
lay my head

her flowers opened
up to me
lifting up

towards my
sun

Warrior-Poet of the Fifth Sun   *Luis A. López*

seeds
of
power

seeds
of
wisdom

planted firmly within

she whispered songs
living
symphonies

the revolving
chorus
of the muse

tlazokamati

Luis A. López

Warrior-Poet of the Fifth Sun

Luis López, born and raised in the diverse population of the Bay Area, now resides in San José, CA.

Born to Mexican parents, López has never been far from the teachings, the ideology nor the spirit of his ancestors.

In his lifetime he as been a musician, a songwriter, a businessman, a technology leader, a father and a friend. Today he is The Warrior-Poet of the Fifth Sun and you'll be pleased that this is so. In these pages López has tapped into a clarity and vision rarely seen in today's poetry. These powerful poems call to mind the revolutionary times of the 60's and 70's while fortifying the path being set by today's poetry giants.

Enjoy.

Victor Espino
author